EDGE OF MEDICINE

MEDICAL ARTIFICIAL INTELLIGENCE

BREAKTHROUGHS

HEATHER E. SCHWARTZ

T0015759

MAYO CLINIC PRESS KIDS

To Philip, Jaz, and Griffin

MAYO CLINIC PRESS KIDS | An imprint of Mayo Clinic Press
200 First St. SW
Rochester, MN 55905
mcpress.mayoclinic.org
To stay informed about Mayo Clinic Press, please subscribe to our free e-newsletter at mcpress.mayoclinic.org or follow us on social media.

For bulk sales to employers, member groups and health-related companies, contact Mayo Clinic at SpecialSalesMayoBooks@mayo.edu.

Proceeds from the sale of every book benefit important medical research and education at Mayo Clinic.

ISBN: 978-1-945564-78-9 (paperback) | 978-1-945564-77-2 (library binding) | 978-1-945564-79-6 (ebook) | 979-8-88770-082-3 (multiuser PDF) | 979-8-88770-081-6 (multiuser ePub)

Library of Congress Control Number: 2022942636
Library of Congress Cataloging-in-Publication Data is available upon request.

TABLE OF CONTENTS

AI AIDS
IN HEALTH CARE

When Cameron Slavens lost his arm in an accident, he got a **prosthetic** limb. Slavens could no longer depend on **nerve** signals from his brain to make arm movements. Instead, he squeezed his muscles in certain patterns to move his arm. Doing this wasn't easy. And it didn't always work.

Then Slavens learned there might be another option. University of Minnesota scientists were researching how **artificial intelligence** (AI) could be used in prosthetics. Slavens reached out to get involved. As part of the program, he tried out a prosthetic arm with AI. To move the arm, all he had to do was think about it. Slavens's brain sent these thoughts as signals to the prosthetic, and the device moved immediately. AI was reading his mind!

When AI is at work, technology can do things humans once believed only other people could do. AI helps scientists research diseases. It helps doctors diagnose them. AI even works directly with patients—all on its own!

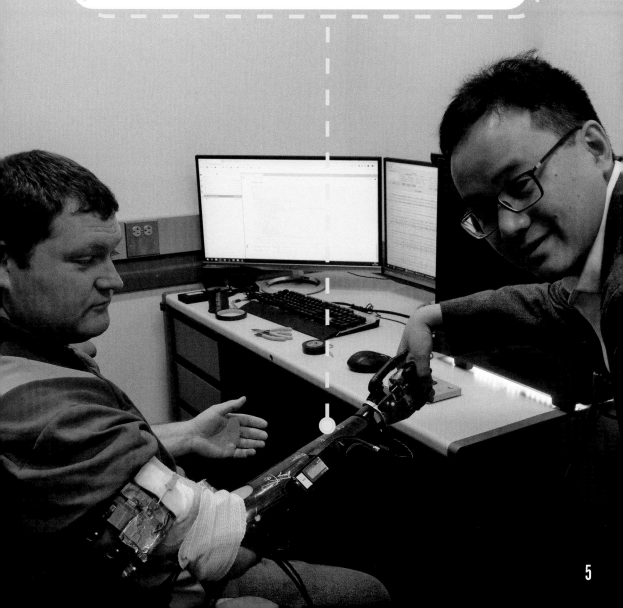

University of Minnesota biomedical engineering professor Zhi Yang (*right*) shakes hands with Cameron Slavens as Slavens tests out the university's robotic arm system.

MEDICINE'S FIRST
AI THERAPIST

Could a computer ever replace a human mental health **therapist**? In 1964, professor Joseph Weizenbaum didn't think so. He even wrote an AI computer program to prove his point.

Weizenbaum named the AI in his program Eliza. He tested it with therapy patients. The patients typed messages to Eliza. Eliza was programmed to pick out key words from these messages. The AI then used those same words to ask the patients questions and keep the conversation going.

Weizenbaum believed patients would be put off by chatting with an emotionless machine. But to his surprise, they really connected with Eliza! The patients shared secrets and held deep conversations with the AI therapist.

Though Weizenbaum hadn't planned on it, he had invented medicine's first AI **chatbot**! In the following decades, Eliza inspired the creation and experimentation of AI programs in health care and other fields.

```
Welcome to
              EEEEEE  LL        IIII   ZZZZZZ   AAAAA
              EE      LL         II        ZZ  AA   AA
              EEEEE   LL         II       ZZZ  AAAAAAA
              EE      LL         II      ZZ    AA   AA
              EEEEEE  LLLLLL   IIII  ZZZZZZ    AA   AA

 Eliza is a mock Rogerian psychotherapist.
 The original program was described by Joseph Weizenbaum in 1966.
 This implementation by Norbert Landsteiner 2005.


ELIZA: Is something troubling you ?
YOU:   Men are all alike.
ELIZA: What is the connection, do you suppose ?
YOU:   They're always bugging us about something or other.
ELIZA: Can you think of a specific example ?
YOU:   Well, my boyfriend made me come here.
ELIZA: Is it important to you that your boyfriend made you come here ?
YOU:   He says I'm depressed much of the time.
ELIZA: I am sorry to hear that you are depressed.
YOU:   It's true. I am unhappy.
ELIZA: Can you explain what made you unhappy ?
YOU:
```

A sample conversation between Eliza and a patient shows how the AI program repeats in its responses key words from the patient's statements. This feature helped users feel understood by and connected to Eliza.

AI DIAGNOSES
DISEASE

Questions doctors seek to answer often relate to diagnoses. *What are the symptoms? What treatment does the patient need?* By the 1970s, US doctor Edward Shortliffe wondered if AI could help answer these questions.

Shortliffe wrote an AI computer program called MYCIN. The program was built to diagnose blood **infections**. Doctors specializing in blood infections were able to diagnose patients. But clinics and hospitals had few specialists. And patients experiencing symptoms visited **general practitioners**, who are less familiar with blood infections. These doctors may refer a patient to a specialist, meaning a second appointment and delayed care.

Enter MYCIN! When doctors used the program, it asked questions, then listed possible diagnoses. Each diagnosis listed reasons it could be correct. MYCIN also recommended treatments. The AI program was just as **accurate** at diagnoses as blood infection specialists were!

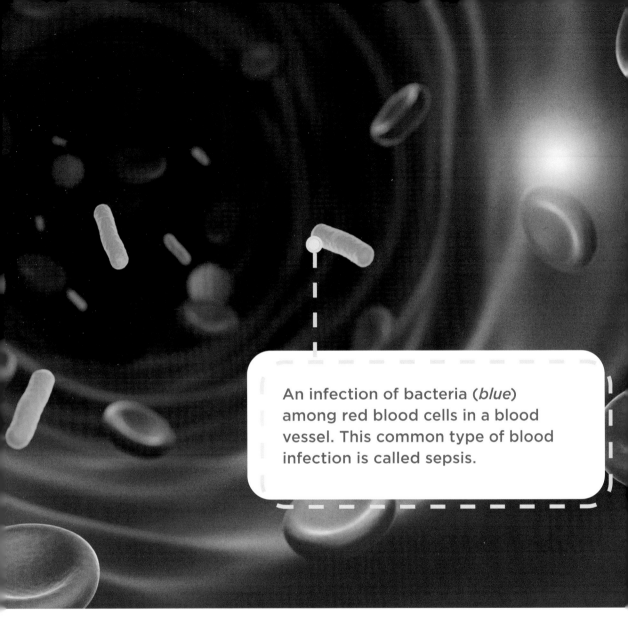

An infection of bacteria (*blue*) among red blood cells in a blood vessel. This common type of blood infection is called sepsis.

In 1986, scientists developed another AI program capable of diagnosing diseases. DXplain had a database of 500 diseases it could diagnose. By 2022, the database had grown to 2,600 diseases! DXplain made it faster and easier for doctors to match symptoms with diagnoses.

ELIZABETH: THE FIRST VIRTUAL NURSE

In 2008, professor Timothy Bickmore led a team at Northeastern University in Massachusetts in creating an AI nurse. First, the team observed human nurses and patients. They learned that patients and nurses made small talk before discussing medical care. Researchers also noticed patients and nurses made movements with their hands and made facial expressions as they spoke.

The Northeastern team used its observations to develop Elizabeth, the world's first virtual nurse. Elizabeth helped discharge patients from the hospital. She was an **avatar** on a screen. Elizabeth had human touches, including hand movements and facial expressions. She was also programmed to make small talk.

Patients liked interacting with Elizabeth. Some even preferred Elizabeth to human nurses since she never made them feel rushed. This **affirmed** one of Elizabeth's main purposes. She could fill in whenever human nurses became busy!

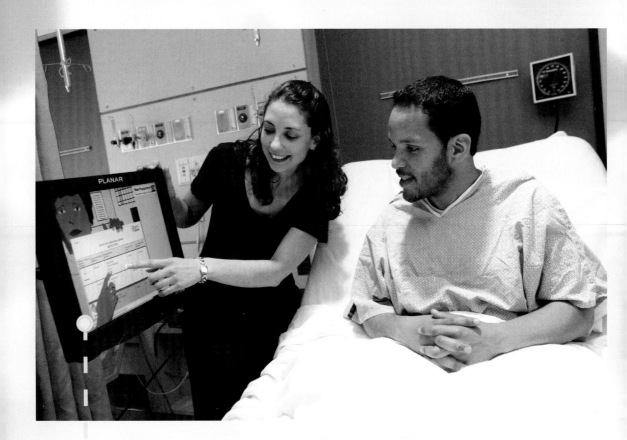

Patients interact with Elizabeth by touchscreen, choosing onscreen options or answers to questions. The patient can also flag any items they don't understand or something they want to discuss further. Then, a human nurse will follow up with the patient on these items.

WATSON: FROM
GAME SHOW TO MAYO CLINIC

In 2011, an AI computer program named Watson went up against champion players on the trivia game show *Jeopardy!* Watson answered questions about literature and science. Show audiences were shocked when it beat its human competitors. What else could Watson do? Researchers at Minnesota's Mayo Clinic decided to find out!

Mayo researchers knew that clinical trials, which offer new and **emerging** treatments, could help **cancer** patients. But it was difficult to match patients with the right trials quickly. Matching involved sifting through a lot of information, including medical **scans** and treatment histories. Mayo doctors hoped Watson could help read and organize this data.

By 2016, Mayo used a special version of Watson to match breast cancer patients with clinical trials more quickly than traditional matching methods. In 2022, the Mayo team continued to explore ways the AI program could help with clinical trials.

Watson appears behind a *Jeopardy!* podium showing its trivia earnings during its 2011 appearance on the show. The screen behind the podium only represented the AI device, which was actually the size of ten refrigerators!

ELLIE:
AI AVATAR

The medical world's first AI therapist, Eliza, was invented in the 1960s. By 2014, mental health care had advanced. And scientists wanted to create an advanced version of Eliza. That year, the USC Institute for Creative Technologies in California introduced the AI program Ellie.

Much like Eliza, Ellie could talk with patients. But she could also do much more! Ellie was a combination of technologies. She was an avatar patients could see onscreen. She had **sensors** to watch and respond to patients' expressions and tone of voice. If a patient looked or sounded sad, Ellie might make a sympathetic gesture.

Ellie also had advantages over human therapists. She never got distracted. Patients could see her no matter where they lived. And her office hours were unlimited.

When patients had to fill out forms about their mental health, they did it. But when they met with Ellie, they revealed more. They opened up to the advanced AI therapist.

A computer screen shows both Ellie (*right*) and her patient (*left*) as Ellie reacts to the patient's body language and voice in real time.

RAFAEL FONSECA, MD

MAYO CLINIC

Q: How can artificial intelligence help doctors fight cancer?

A: AI and machine learning will help integrate all of what we know about a person's cancer, including their biology, health status, logistics, and patient preference, into solutions tailored for each individual. There will be a gradual dismantling of too-general treatment recommendations.

Q: What is the most rewarding part of working in medicine for you?

A: Being able to see how progress and innovation changes and improves lives.

It is a team effort that includes patients, academic centers, and industry. This progress can now be communicated in a much faster fashion and has further reach. The availability of AI will allow Mayo to reach even more of those who need expert care. I love working in cancer treatment, as it embodies the ideal marriage of scientific progress and humanism.

Q: What might the future of medical artificial intelligence look like?

A: The real future will be one in which doctors won't even know they are using AI and yet they will **deliver** best care. AI will be found in many places and will anticipate problems and solutions. AI cannot replace the human aspect of medicine, but it will assure us of best practices being considered.

AI INSIDE
THE BODY

Internal parts of the body are difficult to treat without **surgery**. Enter nanobots! These are AI **microscopic** robots. For decades, scientists have researched using these bots inside living beings. In 2015, University of California scientists began testing to make it a reality!

The scientists **implanted** AI nanobots in a mouse. The bots attached themselves to the mouse's stomach lining. Then they began to **dissolve**. Medicine inside the nanobots was released. The mouse was treated without harm!

Other researchers expanded on this success, working on AI nanobots for humans. In 2017, University of Iowa scientists researched nanobots they hoped would deliver **chemotherapy**. Chemotherapy delivery methods at the time could not target cancer cells. So, the medicine also killed healthy cells, making patients feel very ill. The AI nanobots would target only cancer cells, preventing the ill side effects!

A digital illustration represents the way a nanobot could target and kill cancer cells within the human body.

AI

HEART HELP

Some heart conditions don't show symptoms when they first develop. This can make it difficult for even the most skilled doctors to diagnose these cases. Itzhak Zachi Attia, a machine learning engineer at Minnesota's Mayo Clinic, figured out a way he could help!

Attia studied the heart and different heart conditions. He watched surgeries in action. He sat in on patient exams and gathered data. Then he and a team developed AI that could train computers to review this data. The AI compared the data to patients to find those who might have an emerging heart problem. In 2019, the AI was put to use detecting a weak heart pump in patients.

Attia's work led to Mayo Clinic studies showing that AI interpretation of **electrocardiograms** could detect several heart conditions. One study used AI to screen people without symptoms for risk of a heart condition called **atrial fibrillation**. The AI correctly identified the risk 80 percent of the time!

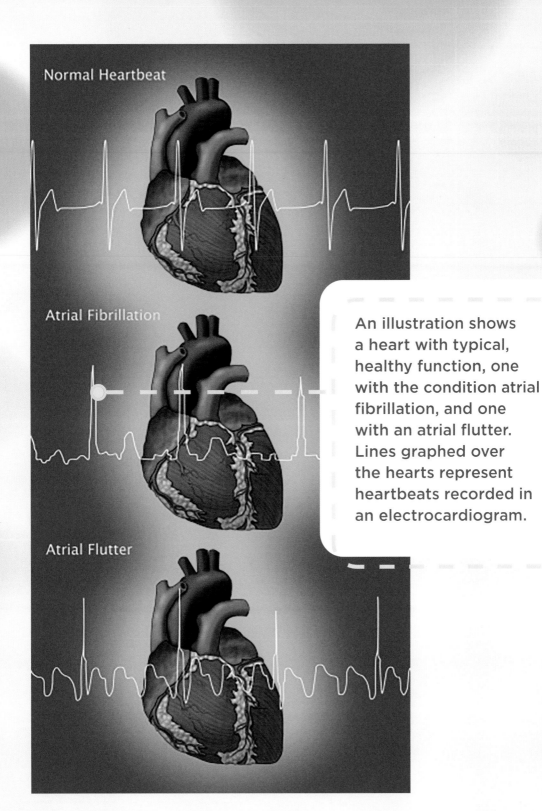

Normal Heartbeat

Atrial Fibrillation

Atrial Flutter

An illustration shows a heart with typical, healthy function, one with the condition atrial fibrillation, and one with an atrial flutter. Lines graphed over the hearts represent heartbeats recorded in an electrocardiogram.

AI IDENTIFIES
PROTEINS AT TOP SPEEDS

Proteins are **molecules** that build, care for, and repair **tissues** in the body. They come in different shapes. Their shape **determines** how a protein acts. Figuring out protein shapes allows scientists to better treat certain diseases.

For decades, scientists used **X-rays** and microscopes to establish protein structures. It often took years of work to figure out a single protein structure this way. As of 2020, AI has learned to do that task—and much more quickly!

Researchers at a company called DeepMind in England looked at existing AI technology. They knew computers could identify faces in a photo. The researchers thought perhaps this capability could be used to identify protein shapes.

DeepMind developed the AI program AlphaFold. The program uses a mathematical system to study data and patterns. Instead of identifying faces in a photo, it identifies known protein shapes. That allows it to predict unknown protein shapes. AlphaFold can establish a protein's shape within minutes!

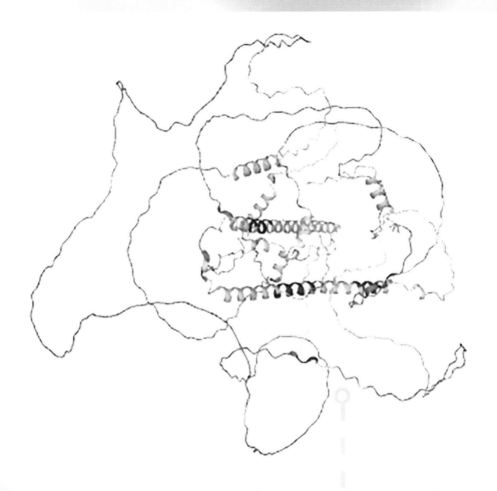

An AlphaFold model displays predicted protein shapes. Each color represents the level of confidence the program has in that area of the predicted shape. Dark blue is the highest level of confidence, followed by light blue, yellow, and orange.

AI DETECTS
EARLY-STAGE CANCER

Pancreatic cancer can be cured if it's treated right away. But treating it early requires an early diagnosis. This can be tricky, as this type of cancer may not cause symptoms in early stages. By the time doctors discover the disease in patients, it is often too late to cure. In 2021, Mayo Clinic wanted to solve this problem. It turned to AI!

Mayo researchers studied the scans of certain patients. These patients did not show pancreatic cancer during the scan. But some had developed the disease later. Others did not. The Mayo team built AI programs to look through these scans and seek patterns in the data to explain why.

The AI figured out which patients without symptoms were likely to develop pancreatic cancer. Mayo's technology allowed its doctors to detect—and treat—the disease early! In 2022, the team started work on a trial of the AI program with 12,500 participants. The trial could lead to early treatment for thousands of people in the future.

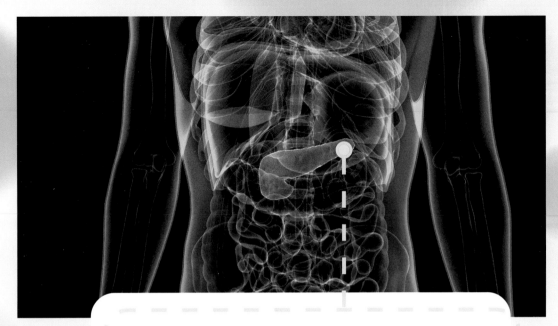

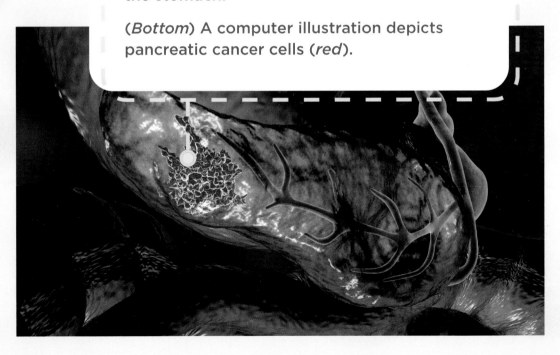

(*Top*) The pancreas is located below the ribs. It sits in front of the spine and behind the stomach.

(*Bottom*) A computer illustration depicts pancreatic cancer cells (*red*).

INCREDIBLE

AI BIONICS

Prosthetic arms, hands, and fingers serve their users best when they are able to move naturally. In 2022, University of Minnesota scientists created an AI system to make this possible.

The scientists implanted an **electrode** where the prosthetic would attach to the user's skin. The electrode captured nerve signals. The brain creates these signals when it thinks about moving a limb or digit. AI inside the electrode was programmed to learn what these signals meant the brain wanted the body to do.

The AI not only learned the **intention** behind each nerve signal. It also learned to turn those signals into action—and within a fraction of a second! That allowed the prosthetic to move almost automatically after the wearer thought about it. In 2021, a team at Ohio's Cleveland Clinic was testing AI limbs to go a step further, providing users with the sense of touch!

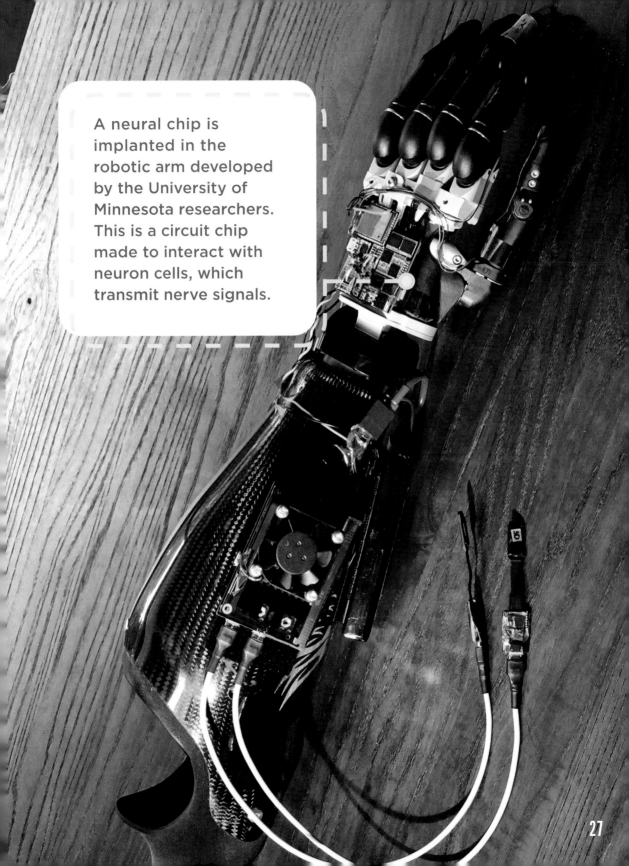

A neural chip is implanted in the robotic arm developed by the University of Minnesota researchers. This is a circuit chip made to interact with neuron cells, which transmit nerve signals.

TIMELINE

1964

Eliza, medicine's first chatbot, helps patients through computerized therapy sessions.

2008

Elizabeth, medicine's first virtual nurse, puts patients at ease by reading facial expressions and other nonverbal cues.

1986

DXplain aids doctors in matching symptoms and test results with possible diagnoses by combing through a large database of diseases.

2014

Ellie is developed as a virtual therapist. The avatar has sensors to monitor patients' expressions and tone of voice.

2016

AI matches breast cancer patients with clinical trials.

2020

Researchers create AlphaFold. The AI determines protein shapes that can lead to the development of more efficient drug treatments.

2019

The Mayo Clinic uses AI to detect heart problems in asymptomatic patients. The AI has an 80 percent success rate.

2022

University of Minnesota scientists develop AI that can read nerve signals, allowing people wearing prosthetics to use thought alone to move the devices!

2017

Scientists research AI nanobots that could someday deliver chemotherapy that won't cause side effects.

2021

The Mayo Clinic develops AI that can detect pancreatic cancer before patients show symptoms.

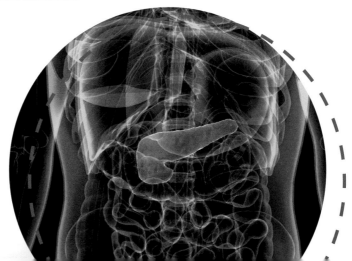

GLOSSARY

accurate—free from mistakes or error

affirm—to confirm something as true

artificial intelligence—an area of computer science focused on giving machines the ability to copy or learn intelligent human behavior

atrial fibrillation—an irregular, often very rapid, heart rhythm that can cause blood clots in the heart

avatar—a small picture that represents a computer character

cancer—a group of often deadly diseases in which harmful cells spread quickly

chatbot—a computer that converses with humans through typed messages or voice commands

chemotherapy—the use of chemicals to treat or control a disease

deliver—to send or bring

determine—to decide firmly

dissolve—when a substance breaks down and mixes with a liquid

electrocardiogram—a record or display of a person's heartbeat produced by electrocardiography

electrode—a conductor through which electricity leaves or enters

emerging—newly created or growing in strength or popularity

general practitioner—a person (especially a doctor) whose work is not limited to a special area

implant—to place something in a person's body during surgery

infection—the entrance and growth of germs in the body

intention—a planned course of action

internal—inside the body

microscope—a device containing a powerful magnifying glass used to see items invisible to the human eye. These items are called microscopic.

molecule—the smallest possible amount of a particular substance that has all the characteristics of that substance

nerve—one of many thin parts that control movement and feeling by carrying messages between the brain and other parts of the body

prosthetic—an artificial body part

scan—an image of a body part, produced using medical technology. To scan is to obtain this image.

sensor—a device that detects or senses heat, light, sound, or motion and then reacts to it

surgery—a medical treatment performed on internal body parts

therapist—a medical professional who cares for patients' mental or physical health through talking or activities. These talks or activities are called therapy.

tissue—a group of like cells that work together in the body to perform a function

X-ray—an image taken using radiation and showing a portion inside the human body

LEARN MORE

Britannica Kids: Artificial Intelligence
https://kids.britannica.com/kids/article/artificial-intelligence/390648

How to Be Good at Science, Technology, and Engineering. London: DK Children, 2018.

Kulz, George Anthony. *Artificial Intelligence in the Real World*. Mendota Heights, Minnesota: Focus Readers, 2020.

Mayo Clinic: Artificial Intelligence and Informatics
https://www.mayo.edu/research/departments-divisions/artificial-intelligence-informatics/overview

National Geographic Kids: Could a Robot Become President?
https://kids.nationalgeographic.com/books/article/could-a-robot-become-president

INDEX

PHOTO ACKNOWLEDGMENTS

ARTUR PLAWGO/Science Source, p. 9; artyway/Shutterstock Images, cover (red, blue abstract); David Gifford/ Science Source, p. 19; Dot Diva/Flickr, pp. 11, 28 (top); Jumper, J et al. Highly accurate protein structure prediction with AlphaFold. Nature (2021). Varadi, M et al. AlphaFold Protein Structure Database: massively expanding the structural coverage of protein-sequence space with high-accuracy models. Nucleic Acids Research (2021), p. 23; KATERYNA KON/Science Source, p. 25 (bottom); Lars Plougmann/Flickr, pp. 15, 28 (bottom); Life science/ Shutterstock Images, pp. 25 (top), 29 (bottom); Mayo Clinic, p. 16; metamorworks/Shutterstock Images, back cover, p. 17; Monica Schroeder/Science Source, p. 21; Naeblys/iStockphoto, cover (head and brain); Neuroelectronics Lab, University of Minnesota, cover, pp. 5, 27; Seth Wenig/AP Images, p. 13; traffic_analyzer/iStockphoto, cover (background); Vladimir Vladimirov/iStockphoto, cover (child and parent); Wikimedia Commons, p. 7